ANNIE S. SWAN

COURTSHIP AND MARRIAGE
AND THE GENTLE ART
OF HOME-MAKING

"Love is the incense that doth sweeten earth."

"Be it ever so humble, There's no place like home."

OMNIA VERITAS

Annie S. Swan
(Mrs. Burnett-Smith)

Courtship and Marriage

and the Gentle Art

of Home-Making

1894

Published by

Omnia Veritas Ltd

Omnia Veritas

www.omnia-veritas.com

TO

The Loved Memory

OF

MY FATHER.

"An honest man—the noblest work of God."

I. THE LOVERS

O f this truly gentle art we do not hear a great deal. It has no academies connected with its name, no learned body of directors or councillors, no diplomas or graduation honours; yet curiously enough it offers more enduring consequences than any other art which makes more noise in the world. Its business is the most serious business of life, fraught with the mightiest issues here and hereafter—viz., the moulding of human character and the guiding of human conduct. It is right and fitting, then, that it should demand from us some serious attention, and we may with profit consider how it can best be fostered and made competent to bless the greatest number, which, I take it, is the *ultima Thule* of all art. To trace this gentle art from its early stages we must first consider, I think, the relation to each other before marriage of the young pair who aim at the upbuilding of a home, wherein they shall not only be happy themselves, but which, in their best moments, when the heavenly and the ideal is before them, they hope to make a centre of influence from which shall go forth means of grace and blessing to others.

I do not feel that any apology is required for my desire to linger a little over that old-fashioned yet ever-new phase of life known as courting days. It is one which is oftener made a jest of than a serious study; yet such is its perennial freshness and interest for men and women, that it can never become threadbare; and though there cannot be much left that is new or original to say about it, yet a few thoughts from a woman's point of view may not be altogether unacceptable. We are constantly being told that we live in a hard, prosaic age, that romance has no place in our century, and that the rush and the fever of life have left but little time or inclination for the old-time grace and leisure with which our grandfathers and grandmothers loved, wooed, and wed.

This study of human nature is my business, and it appears to me that the world is very much as it was—that Eden is still possible to those who are fit for it; and it is beyond question that love, courtship, and marriage are words to conjure with in the garden of youth, and that a love-story has yet the power to charm even sober men and women of middle age, for whom romance is mistakenly supposed to be over.

Every man goes to woo in his own way, and the woman he woos is apt to think it the best way in the world; it would be superfluous for a mere outsider to criticise it. Examples might be multiplied; in the novels we read we have variety and to spare. We know the types well. Let me enumerate a few. The diffident youth, weighed down with a sense of his own unworthiness, approaching his divinity with a blush and a stammer; and in some extreme cases—these much affected by the novelists of an earlier decade—going down upon his knees; the bold wooer, who believes in storming the citadel, and is visited by no misgiving qualms; the cautious one, who counts the cost, and tries to make sure of his answer beforehand,—the only case in which I believe that a woman has a right to exercise the qualities of the coquette; then we have also the victim of extreme shyness, who would never come to the point at all without a little assistance from the other side. There are other types,—the schemer and the self-seeker, whose matrimonial ventures are only intended to advance worldly interests. We need not begin to dissect them—it would not be a profitable occupation.

Well, while not seeking or attempting to lay down rules or offer any proposition as final, there are sundry large and general principles which may be touched upon to aid us in looking at this interesting subject from a sympathetic and common-sense point of view.

Most people, looking back, think their own romance the most beautiful in the world, even if it sometimes lacked that dignity which the onlooker thought desirable.

It is a crisis in the life of a young maiden when she becomes conscious for the first time that she is an object of special interest to a member of the opposite sex; that interest being conveyed in a thousand delicate yet unmistakable ways, which cause a strange flutter at her heart, and make her examine her own feelings to find whether there be a responsive chord. The modest, sensible, womanly girl, who is not yet extinct, in spite of sundry croakers, will know much better than anybody can tell her how to adjust her own conduct at this crisis in her life. Her own innate delicacy and niceness of perception will guide her how to act, and if the attentions be acceptable to her she will give just the right meed of encouragement, so that the course of true love may run smoothly towards consummation. Of course the usual squalls and cross currents must be looked for—else would that delightful period of life be robbed of its chief zest and charm, to say nothing of the unhappy novelist's occupation, which would undoubtedly be gone for ever.

There have occasionally been discussions as to the desirability of long engagements, and there are sufficient arguments both for and against; but the best course appears to be, as in most other affairs of life, to try and strike the happy medium. Of necessity, circumstances alter cases. When the young pair have known each other for a long period of years, and there are no obstacles in the way, the long engagement is then superfluous.

But in cases where an attachment arises out of a very brief acquaintance, I should think it desirable that some little time should be given for the pair to know something of each other before incurring the serious responsibility of life together. Of course it is true that you cannot thoroughly know a person till you live with him or her; yet it is surely possible to form a fair estimate of personal character before entering on that crucial ordeal, and there is no doubt that fair opportunity given for such estimate considerably reduces the matrimonial risk. That the risk is great and serious even the most giddy and thoughtless will not deny. No doubt both men and maidens are on their best behaviour during courting days; still, if a mask be worn, it must of necessity sometimes be drawn aside, and a glimpse of the real personality obtained.

It is not for me to say what should or should not be the conduct of a young man during his period of probation, though of course I may be allowed my own ideas concerning it.

One thing, however, is very sure, and that is, that if he truly and whole-heartedly love the woman he desires to make his wife, this pure and ennobling passion, which I believe to be a "means of grace" to every man, will arouse all that is best and purest and highest in him,—that is, if the woman be worthy his regard, and capable of exercising such an influence over him. It is possible for a man to deteriorate under the constant companionship of a light-minded, frivolous woman, who by force of her personal attractions and fascinations can keep him at her side, even against his better judgment. But only for a time: the woman who has beauty only, and does not possess those lasting qualities, stability of mind and purity of heart, will not long retain her hold upon the affections she has won. I will do men credit to believe that they desire something more in a wife than mere physical attractions, though these are by no means to be despised. I am sure every unmarried man hopes to find in the wife he may yet marry a companion and a sympathiser, who will wear the same steadfast and lovely look on grey days as well as gold.

I once heard a young Scotch working man give his definition of a good wife—"A woman who will be the same to you on off-Saturday as pay Saturday." Nor was he very wide of the mark. I have no sort of hesitation in laying down a law for the guidance of young women during that halcyon time "being engaged." She knows very well, without any telling from me, that her influence is almost without limit. In these days before marriage the haunting fear of losing her is before her lover's mind, making him at once humble and pliable, and it is then that the wise, womanly girl sows the seed which will bear rich harvest in the more prosaic days of married life, when many engrossing cares are apt to wean her from the finer shading of higher things.

And here I would wish to emphasise one inexorable fact, which is too often passed by or made light of. I do not set it down in a bitter or pessimistic spirit, but simply stating what men and women of larger experience know to be true: what a man will not give up for a woman before marriage, he never will after. Therefore no young girl can make a more profound mistake than to marry a man of doubtful habits in the hope of reforming him after she is his wife. The reformation must be begun, if not ended before, or the risks are perilous indeed. She will probably repent her folly in sadness and tears. And here I would protest, and solemnly, against that view, held by some women, I believe, though I hope they are few: that a man is none the worse for having been a little fast. It is a most dangerous creed, and one which has done much to lower the morals of this and other days. Let us reverse the position, and ask whether any man in his right mind will admit as much in regarding the woman he would make his wife. If it is imperative that she should be blameless and pure, let him see to it that his record also is clean—that he is fit to mate with her. And I would implore the mistaken and foolish girls who entertain an idea so false to every principle of righteousness and purity to put it from them for ever, and exact from the men to whom they give themselves so absolutely and irrevocably, a standard of purity as high as that set for them. I speak strongly on this subject because it is one on which I feel so very strongly. There is no necessity for priggishness or preaching; the womanly woman, true to the highest ideal, the ideal which God has set for her, can surround herself with that atmosphere, indescribable, undefinable, but in the presence of which impurity and lightness of speech or behaviour cannot live. I believe women are our great moral teachers—would that more of them would awaken to the stupendous greatness of their calling!

Love is the most wonderful educator in the world; it opens up worlds and possibilities undreamed of to those to whom it comes, the gift of God. I am speaking of love which is worthy of the name, not of its many counterfeits. The genuine article only, based upon respect and esteem, can stand the test of time, the wear and tear of life; the love which is the wine of life, more stimulating and more heart-inspiring when the days are dark than at any other time,—the love which rises to the occasion, and which many waters cannot quench.

Blessed be God that it is still as possible to us men and women of to-day as to the pair that dwelt in Eden!

II. THE IDEAL WIFE

Now having brought our young pair so far on the road, we must needs go a step farther, and see what grit is in them for the plain prose of daily life; not that we admit or hint for a moment that poetry must be laid aside, only the prose may, very likely will, demand their first consideration. If the novels most eagerly read, most constantly sought after at the libraries and book-shops, are any sign of the times, we may feel very certain that marriage has caused no diminution of interest in those looking on, but rather the reverse, so we may follow them without hesitation across the threshold of their new home.

And as the wife is properly supposed to be the light and centre of the home, we must first consider her position in it, and her fitness for it. It is by no means so easy to fill the position successfully as the uninitiated are apt to suppose; and I have no hesitation in saying that the first year of married life is a crucial test of a woman's disposition and character. It brings out her individuality in bold relief, shows her at her worst and best. She has to give herself so entirely and unreservedly, and in many cases to merge her individuality in that of another, that to do it with grace requires a considerable drain on her fund of unselfishness. It is even more difficult in cases where the wife has come from a home where she was idolised, and perhaps indulged a great deal more than was good for her.

It seems to me that one of the most valuable qualities the new wife can take with her is unselfishness. Equipped with that, everything else will come easily.

While it is true that she is required, to a certain extent, sometimes greater and sometimes less, to take a back place, she must be careful not to lose her individuality, to become merely an echo of her husband, to render herself insipid. It is a fine distinction, perhaps, but necessary to observe, because I am sure there is no man here present, married or unmarried, or anywhere else, unless a fool, who would wish to be tied for life to a nonentity.

The woman who dearly loves her husband will never seek to usurp his place as head of the house; nay, she will delight to keep herself in the background if by so doing he can show to more advantage. Even if nature has endowed her with gifts more richly than her spouse, she will be careful, out of the very wealth of her love, not to make the contrast observable.

It has been said that men prefer as wives women whose intelligence is not above the average; but is that not a libel on the sex? The higher the intelligence the more satisfactory the performance of the duties required of a reasonable being; and I would therefore insist that the woman of large brain power, provided she has well-balanced judgment, and a heart as expansive as her brain, will more nearly approach the ideal in matrimony than the more frivolous woman, who has no thought beyond her personal aggrandisement and adornment, and who buys her new bonnet with a kiss.

The woman who looks with intelligent interest upon the large questions affecting the welfare of the world is likely to bring a more wide and loving sympathy to bear upon the concerns of more immediate moment to her, and which affect the welfare of all within the walls of her home.

I am old-fashioned enough to think these latter should be her first concern, but in her large heart she may have room for many more; for when the outlook is narrow and mean, when nothing is deemed of consequence except what affects self and those circled by selfish interest, life becomes a poor thing, and human nature a stunted and miserable quality. I have known, as, I daresay, you also have known, women whose whole talk is "my home," "my husband," "my children," until one grows weary of the selfish iteration, and prays to be delivered from it.

We have of late years had much amusing and perhaps, in some remote degree, profitable newspaper discussion on the subject of married life, and the respective merits of wives. On the whole, the wife, I think, has fared but badly at the hands of her critics. She is a great grievance to some, it would appear, from the minuteness with which her faults and failings have been enumerated. That she may have her uses has been somewhat grudgingly admitted; that she may in some rare instances sweeten the desert of life for her mate is not absolutely denied; but in the main she is judged to have fallen short—in a word, she is *not* ideal. Of course such discussion and such verdict is but the froth on a passing wave; still, it serves to illustrate my contention that there is no subject on earth of more surpassing interest to men and women than this very theme we are considering. The men who have written on the subject lay great stress on a loving disposition and an amiable temper, which are indeed two most powerful factors in the scene of wedded happiness. An amiable temper is a gift of God which cannot be too highly prized, since those who have it not must be constantly at war with self. When combined with these sweet qualities is a large meed of common sense, which accepts the inevitable, even if it bring disappointment and disillusionment in its train, with a cheerful philosophy, then is the happiness of married life secured. The buffets of fortune cannot touch it—its house is builded on a rock.

It is Lady Henry Somerset, I think, who has said that sentimentality has been from time immemorial the curse of woman. There is a great deal of truth in the remark. We want women to be delivered from this sickly thrall of sentimentality—which word I use as distinct from sentiment, a very different quality indeed; we desire them to take wider, healthier, sounder views of life.

In fiction it is no longer considered necessary to bring one's heroine to the very verge of a decline in order to make her interesting; and nobody now has much sympathy with Thackeray's favourite Amelia, and other limp young women who are dissolved in tears on the smallest provocation, sometimes on none at all.

No, we want a more robust womanhood than that, sound of body and sound of mind, in order that our homes may be happy and well regulated, our children born and reared fit for the battle of life. A well-known novelist, lecturing recently on the younger generation of fiction-writers, remarked that Robert Louis Stevenson, in ignoring woman so much in his works, had passed by the most picturesque part of human life. The contention was perfectly unimpeachable from the artistic point of view; but we aim, I trust, at being something more than picturesque. While not disdaining the high privilege of giving the romance and sweetness to life, we would desire also to be strong, capable, serviceable to our day and generation. So and so only can we hope to be the equal and the friend of man. But in this worthy aim we have to steer clear of many quicksands; we must avoid the very semblance of usurpation or imitation.

Surely we are sufficiently endowed with our own gifts and graces, so powerful in their influence, that I need not enumerate or expatiate upon them here.

Let us not forget that in true womanliness is our strength, and that the end of our being is to comfort and bless and love—never to usurp.

What can be more melancholy than to live with a grumbler, to sit opposite a face prematurely wrinkled at the brows and down-drooped at the lips? I have in my mind's eye, as perhaps you have in yours, such a woman, tied to the best of good fellows, who, through no fault of his own, has not as yet made such headway in life as was expected of him. And his Nemesis sits at home, querulous and fretful because her establishment is more modest than her ambition, her possessions than her pretensions. Life is embittered to him; hope has died: if love follow it sadly to the bier, who can blame him? Certainly not the woman who has been a hindrance and not a help, one whose reproaches, tacit and acknowledged, have caused the iron to enter into his soul. It is such women who send men to mental and moral destruction, nor is their punishment lacking.

The ideal wife, then, will sedulously cultivate the happy spirit of contentment, and make the best of everything, not seeking to add to the burden an already overworked husband may have to carry. It is not the abundance of worldly possessions which makes happiness. I can speak from personal experience, and I could tell you a story of a young pair who began life in very humble circumstances, in the face of much opposition, and who, by dint of honest, faithful, united endeavours, overcame obstacles over which Experience shook her head and called insurmountable. And the struggle being over, the memory of it is sweet beyond all telling,—the little shifts to make ends meet, the constant planning and striving, the simple pleasures won by waiting and hard work, are possessions which they would not barter for untold gold.

The woman who loves and is beloved finds herself strong to bear the ills that may meet her from day to day. We have much to bear physically, and it is hard to carry always a bright spirit in a frail body; but we have our compensations, which are many. They will at once occur to every sympathetic and discerning heart, but are they not after all summed up in the eloquent words of Holy Writ, "The heart of her husband doth safely trust in her;" "Her children arise and call her blessed"?

And these, after all, are the heavenliest gifts for women here below, and the wise woman, so blessed, will always feel that her possessions are greater than her needs, and in her loving service, for her own first, and afterwards for all whom her blessed influence can reach, will as near as possible approach the ideal. With God, tender to Woman always, we may safely leave the rest.

III. THE IDEAL

HUSBAND

The duties and obligations of the husband in the house are surely not less binding than those of the wife; he has to contribute his share towards its happiness or misery. The ideal husband, from a woman's point of view, is a many-sided creature; but his outstanding characteristic must of necessity be his power to make the home of which he is the head come as near to the heavenly type as may be in this mundane sphere. However wise and wifely and absolutely conscientious in her endeavour the wife may be, she cannot unaided make the perfect home—it must be a joint concern. The pity of it is we so often see two, bound together by the closest and most indissoluble of all earthly ties, walking their separate ways, forgetful of both spirit and letter of their marriage vows. This home-making and home-keeping quality is the very wherefore of the man's existence as a husband; for his home with its shelter, adequate or inadequate, is all he has to offer in exchange for the woman who has given him herself. If she be cheated of her birthright here, she may consider herself poor indeed.

There are undoubtedly very many selfish and purely self-seeking women, who starve the atmosphere about them; but as a rule the beauty of true unselfishness is oftener found adorning the female character than the male. Nobody attempts to deny this, therefore when we meet a truly unselfish man we must regard him with reverence, as a being truly great. It is without doubt a more arduous task for a man to cultivate the unselfish spirit, because the training of the race for centuries has rather tended to the fostering of selfishness in him—woman having for long been cheated of her lawful place and power in the scheme of creation.

The quality most of all admired by woman in man is manliness: she can forgive almost anything but his lack of courage.

The manly man, conscious of his strength, is of necessity tender and considerate towards those weaker than himself, and so wins their confidence and love. When he marries, therefore, he takes a wife to shield her from the rude blasts of the world; all that his care and tenderness can do will be done to make lighter for her the ordinary burdens of life. Nor will he expect impossibilities, nor growl because he finds he has married a very human woman, with a great many needs and wants. Angels do not mate with mortals, the contrast would be too one-sided.

It is well with the man who has in his wife not only a bright companion for his days of sunshine, but who in the crises of his life finds in her heart the jewel of common sense and the pearl of a quick understanding. The wife who comprehends him at once when he says expenditure has been too heavy, that it must be reduced to meet the altered finances, and who not only comprehends, but cheerfully acquiesces, planning with him how retrenchment can best be carried out; the wife to whom the lack of the new bonnet or the new carpet is a matter of small moment,—she it is who makes glad the heart of her husband. Ay, but what kind of a husband? He must first deserve this jewel before he can expect her to display those qualities which money cannot buy, but which prevent marriage from being the failure sundry croakers would have us believe. How is he to deserve her? how win her to this most desirable height of perfection? By treating her as an entirely reasonable being, which most women are, in spite of many affirmations to the contrary.

The monetary basis of the engagement matrimonial is not, unfortunately, always sound. How common it is for a man to keep his wife in utter ignorance of the state of his affairs, thus depriving her of the only safe guide she can have in the conduct of her domestic affairs! If a woman is to be a man's true helpmeet, she must stand shoulder to shoulder with him in everything, sharing as far as is possible his anxieties and his hopes, and by judicious expenditure of his means aiding him to the best position it is possible for him to attain. Of course there are poor silly creatures fit to be wife to no man, who do not deserve and could not appreciate confidence, and who are lamentably ignorant of the value of £ *s. d.* But the majority of wives, I would hope, possess sufficient common sense to comprehend the simple questions of income and expenditure when candidly placed before them. How delightful, as well as imperative, to go into a committee of ways and means periodically, talking over everything confidentially, and feeling the sweet bond of union growing closer and dearer because of the cares and worries none can escape, though love and sympathy can make them light!

There is a type of husband—unfortunately rather common—who begrudges his wife, whatever her character and disposition, every penny she spends, even though it is spent primarily for his own comfort, and who has never in his life cheerfully opened out to her his purse, whatever he may have done with the thing he calls his heart. This is a very serious matter, and one which presses heavily on the hearts of many wives. It is hard for a young girl, who may in her father's house have had pocket money always to supply her simple needs, to find herself after marriage practically penniless— having to ask for every penny she requires, and often to explain minutely how and where it is to be spent. I have known a man who required an absolute account of every halfpenny spent by his wife, and who took from her change of the shilling he had given her for a cab fare. We must pray, for the credit of the sex, that there are few so lost to all gentlemanly feeling, to speak of nothing else; but it is certain that, through thoughtlessness as much as stinginess often, many sensitive women suffer keenly from this form of humiliation. It ought not to be. If a woman is worthy to be trusted with a man's honour, which is supposed to be more valuable to him than his gold, let her likewise be trusted with a little of the latter, without having to crave it and answer for it as a servant sent on an errand counts out the copper change to her master on her return. There are many little harmless trifles a woman wants, many small kindnesses she would do on the impulse of the moment, had she money in her purse; and though she may sometimes not be altogether wise, she is blessed in the doing, and nobody is the poorer. However small a man's income, there are surely a few odd shillings the wife might have for her very own, if only to gratify her harmless little whims, and to make her feel that she sometimes has a penny to spare. It is quite desirable, I think, that there should be, even where means are limited (I am not of course alluding to working people whose weekly wage is barely sufficient for family needs), some arrangement whereby the wife may have something, however small, upon which she can depend, and which she can spend when and how she pleases.

Some indulgent fathers, foreseeing the possibility of their daughters feeling the lack of a little money, continue their allowance to their married daughters; but there are very few husbands, one would think, who would care to leave their wives so dependent for little luxuries it should be their privilege to supply.

The labourer is surely worthy of his hire; and the wife, upon whose shoulders the domestic load presses most heavily, is as justly entitled to her payment as her housemaid, whose duties are more clearly defined. Some high-flown personages may think this a very gross view of the case, and say, perchance, that where love is there can never be any hardship felt. But I know that I touch upon what is a sore point with many women, and I can only hope that if any stingy husbands read these words they will try a little experiment on their own account, and see how the unexpected gift of a little money, offered lovingly, can bring the light back to eyes which have grown a little weary, and smooth the lines away from a brow which care has wrinkled before its time.

The ideal husband we are considering will also be a home-keeping husband. Let me not here be misunderstood. No sensible woman will desire to keep her husband always at her side, nor can any woman make a more profound mistake than to try and wean the man she has married away from all his old friends and associations. I am speaking of good men, of course, whose friends and associations are such as she need not regard with apprehension. Yet it is a mistake which many women make, and it is a common saying with the bachelors who may miss a certain bright spirit from their midst, "Oh, nobody ever sees him now, he's married!" And there is a peculiar emphasis on the last word which you must hear to appreciate, but it signifies that he is as good as dead.

Now why should this be? The wise wife, instead of being so small-minded and jealous, should try to remember that there is a side of man's nature which demands sympathy and contact with his own sex—

and also that her husband knew and loved these old friends of his perhaps before he ever saw her. Let her try instead to make them all so welcome in her home that they will come and come again, and instead of pitying her husband because he has got his head into a noose will go away thinking him a lucky fellow. This is not an impossibility. It can be done.

But while this husband of ours does not give up his old friends of his own sex, nor abjure all the manly pursuits and recreations so dear to his soul in his state of bachelorhood, he will take care that they do not absorb an undue share of his leisure, but will prefer home and wife to them all, and *let her know it*. He will not be above expressing his satisfaction when his home suddenly strikes him with more force than usual as being the sweetest place on earth; he will say so just as frankly as he finds fault when there is just cause for complaint; and she will return it by a loving interest pressed down and running over, or I am neither woman nor wife.

The ideal husband, then, is no more perfect than the ideal wife; nor would she wish him to be other than he is, manly, generous, kindly-hearted, well-conditioned, and, above all things, true as steel. That he occasionally loses his temper, and does many thoughtless and stupid things, makes no difference so long as his heart is pure and tender and true.

The ideal relationship betwixt husband and wife has always appeared to me to be comradeship,—a standing shoulder to shoulder, upholding each other through thick and thin, and above all keeping their inner sanctuary sacred from the world.

41

What says one of our greatest teachers in "Romola"?—"She who willingly lifts the veil from her married life transforms it from a sanctuary into a vulgar place." These are solemn words, solemn and true. We have in these strange days too much publicity—the fierce light beats not only on the throne but on the humbler home. The craving for details relating to the private life of those who may in any degree stand out among their fellows has developed into a species of disease. Kept within due bounds this curiosity is in itself harmless, and may be to a certain extent gratified, but the privacy of domestic life cannot be too sacredly guarded; the home ought to be to tired men and women a veritable sanctuary where they can be at peace.

IV. THE FIRST YEAR OF MARRIED LIFE

This is the crucial period in the lives of most married people; the test which decides the wisdom or the folly of the step they have taken. Now, when the irrevocable words have been said, the vow taken for better or for worse, and the door shut upon the outside world, if any mask has been worn it is laid aside and true self revealed. To some this means disillusionment, and disappointment is inevitable, since marriage is entered on from a great variety of motives, and love is not always the first and most potent. With these, meanwhile, we do not propose to deal; their punishment is certain, since there can be no misery on earth more hopeless and more galling than the misery of a loveless marriage.

But even ordinary happy and sensible people, who have married for love, and who honestly desire to make their home as far as possible an earthly paradise, cannot escape the inevitable strain of this first year of married life. To begin with, it is a trite saying that you cannot know a person until you live with him or her; and people come to years of maturity have formed habits of thought and action which may, in some cases must, clash with those of the other with whom they are brought into contact every day. Contact, too, from which it is impossible to escape. You meet in business and society many persons with whom you find it difficult to agree, whose opinions jar upon you, and who rub you the wrong way, and you find it irksome enough to meet such a person even occasionally; imagine, then, what it would be like were you placed in, or forced to endure, his or her companionship every day. Yet such is the experience of some married persons, who have rushed into matrimony without due knowledge or consideration.

But leaving these extreme cases out of the question, meanwhile let us think of the test of perpetual companionship as applied to an ordinary pair who enter on married life with the ordinary prospect of happiness.

During the days of courtship and engagement they, of course, saw a good deal of each other, and got to know, as they thought, every peculiarity and characteristic. Sometimes, even, they had quarrels arising out of trifles, foolish misunderstandings which caused serious heart-burnings, none of which, however, were of long duration; and the making up was invariably sweet enough to atone for the temporary misery, and help to make up the poetry of life. But the lovers' quarrel and the quarrel matrimonial are entirely different; and while the former is usually but a passing breeze, the latter is more serious, and to be avoided almost at any cost. We want fair winds always, if possible, to speed our matrimonial barque; we do not wish its timbers shaken by the whirlwind of passion.

We have all our little peculiarities, excrescences of character which are apt to rub roughly against our neighbours' sensibilities, let us not, when feeling these drawbacks, forget our own. We are so apt to magnify in others, and to minimise in ourselves.

It is easy to be on good behaviour with a person we only see occasionally, even every day, so long as the cares and worries of life are in the background, never obtruded, however heavily they press, because these short moments are too precious to be clouded in any way. It is easy to be unselfish for a little while; to bow, now and then, absolutely to another's will; to suffer discomfort once a week, if necessary, to make a dear one comfortable. All such little sacrifices during courting days seem but a privilege, and make up the poetry of that happy time.

But the day comes sooner or later to the married pair, when the prose pages must be turned, and poetry relegated to the background, days on which the reality of life, in all its grim nakedness, seems to banish romance, and when love needs all its strength and staying power for the fight. The common-sense man or woman, of which type a few examples yet remain with us, will prepare themselves for the slight disappointments which are inevitable, when two people, regarding each other from an adoring distance, and having invested each other with many exaggerated gifts and graces, put themselves voluntarily to the test of everyday life, with all its prosaic details, its crosses and losses, its silences and its tears. It is like making a new acquaintance, having to meet each other in all situations, and in various unromantic and sometimes supremely trying conditions. Edwin pacing his chamber floor anathematising a buttonless shirt is a picture our comic journals have made familiar to us; and Angelina in her curl-papers and untidy morning gown looks a different being from the sylph in evening attire all smiles and blushes. These extreme examples serve only to illustrate my contention, that the closeness of the marriage relation carries its peril with it. To the man or woman, however, who marries for that love which is based on the qualities of both head and heart, and who knows that daily life, with its rubs and scrubs, will sometimes mar the sweetest temper and cloud the serenest brow, there cannot come any serious disillusionment. Loving each other dearly, they remember they are but human; and as perfection is not inborn in humanity, they accept each other's faults and shortcomings gracefully, not magnifying them sourly and grumblingly, but bearing with them, and rejoicing in and accepting the good.

Domestic life to the young and untried housekeeper is something of an ordeal. She may have had her own place in her father's home, her own special duties to attend to, even her own share of responsibility. Still, it is an altogether different matter to have the entire care of a household, to guide all its concerns, and be responsible for the domestic comfort of all within the four walls of the house. Happy the young wife who had a wise mother, and came well-equipped from the parental home.

There is no more fruitful source of the disappointment and disillusionment of which we have been speaking than incapacity on the part of the young wife to steer the domestic boat. All men like creature comforts, and are more keenly sensible perhaps than women to the advantages of a well-ordered home. We all know how women living alone are apt to neglect themselves in the matter of preparing regular and substantial meals; and how many suffer thereby. A good dinner is more to a man than it is to a woman; and, for my part, I do not see why it should be necessary to sneer at a man because he desires and can enjoy a wholesome, well-cooked meal. It is a sign of a healthy body and a sound mind, and the true housewife is never happier than when she caters successfully for the members of her household, and beholds the hearty appreciation of her labours.

It is the custom in certain quarters in these days to decry this special department of woman's work, and to belittle its importance, but I am old-fashioned enough to hold that one of the most essential points of fitness for the married life in woman is her ability to keep house economically, wisely, and successfully. Nothing will ever convince me that such fitness is not one of her solemn and binding duties; in fact, it is one of the reasons of her existence as a wife.

Sometimes her worries and perplexities, at first, resting entirely on her shoulders, may give to her tongue an unusually sharp edge, and she may find it a too serious effort to smile just when her spouse may think it right and fitting that she should.

Out of what trifles do great issues arise! Let not the sun go down upon your wrath. My advice to the young wife when things do *not* go well with her, when she grows hot and tired over a weary dinner, which does not turn out the success she wishes, or when she has been tried beyond all patience with her "help",—my advice is, Don't nag. Be cheerful. Swallow the pill in the kitchen at any cost, but, above all, don't nag! A man will stand almost anything but nagging. Don't save up a long string of miseries, small and big, to pour on to him the moment he puts his head in at the door.

Yes, I know all about it—that the day has been long and dreary, that nothing has gone right, and you have had nobody to share it; but I want you to let the man have his dinner or his tea in peace before you relate the tale of your woes. It will make all the difference in the world to his reception of it. Try to remember that he has had a long day too, that, maybe, he has been nagged and worried in the office, or the market, or behind the counter; and that he left it with relief, hoping for a little fireside comfort at home. Let him enjoy first, at least, the meal you have prepared or superintended, then, when you both have eaten, you will be in a better mood for the discussion of the little worries which looked so big and black all day. If they have not disappeared altogether by this time they have at least sensibly decreased in size and number.

Another thing I should like to impress on the young wife, and that is the absolute necessity of being as fastidious and dainty with her personal appearance after marriage as before. It is a poor compliment to a man to show that you care so little for his opinion as a husband that you can't or won't take the trouble to dress up for him. Dear girls, contemplating the final leap, I want you to understand that you can afford a great deal less to be careless after marriage than before; because you have now to keep the husband you have won. Men like what is bright and cheerful, and pleasant to behold. So far as you are concerned see that you are never an eyesore. Even if you have your own work to do, there is no necessity why you should be a dowdy or a slattern.

Even a cotton dress clean and daintily made can be as becoming to you as a robe of silk and lace.

It is a great deal more important for you to keep your husband's love and respect than it was to win them as a lover; because now your stake is greater—in fact, it is your all.

To the husband I would say, "Be kind, be true, be appreciative always. If you have to find fault do it gently. There are two ways of doing and saying everything. Take time to choose the better, the kinder, the more helpful and encouraging."

Most women are quick to respond to the slightest touch of kindness, the sunshine their more dependent natures require. See that you, having taken this young creature from the shelter of a loving parental home, do not starve her in an atmosphere of cold criticism and fault-finding. Remember that she is young, inexperienced, ignorant of many things, and that wisdom walks with years. Little things these, you say? Yes, friend, but great and far-reaching in their issues even to the wreck or salvation of a human soul.

To both in the early days, "Live near to God,"—His blessing alone can consecrate the home. So will your last days be better than your first, and love be as sweet and soul-satisfying on the brink of the grave, at the close of the long pilgrimage you have made together, as in the halcyon days, "when all the world was young."

V. THE IDEAL HOME

A house is not a home, although it has sometimes to pass as such. There are imposing mansions, replete with magnificence and luxury, which if realised would provide the outward trappings of many modest domiciles, but which offer shelter and nothing more to their possessors.

Home is made by those who dwell within its walls, by the atmosphere they create; and if that spirit which makes humble things beautiful and gracious be absent, then there can be no home in the full and true sense of the word.

While each member of the household contributes more or less to the upbuilding of the fabric, it is, of course, those at the head whose influence makes or mars. A lesser influence may be felt in a degree great enough to modify disagreeable elements, or intensify happy ones, but it cannot, save in very exceptional circumstances, set aside the influence of those at the head.

It is to them, then, that our few words under this heading must be addressed; and, to reduce it to a still narrower basis, it is the woman's duty and privilege, and solemn responsibility, which make this art of home-making more interesting and important to her than any other art in the world. Her right to study it, and to make it a glorious and perfect thing, will never be for a moment questioned, even in this age of fierce rivalry and keen competition for the good things of life. In her own kingdom she may make new laws and inaugurate improvements without let or hindrance, and as a rule she will meet with more gratitude and appreciation than usually fall to the lot of law-givers and law-makers. She will also find in her own domain scope for her highest energies, and for the exercise of such originality as she may be endowed with. I do not know of any sphere with a wider scope, but of course it requires the open eye and the understanding heart to discern this fact.

It seems superfluous, after the chapters preceding this, to say again that the very first principle to be learned in this art of home-making must be love. Without it the other virtues act but feebly. There may be patience, skill, tact, forbearance, but without true love the home cannot reach its perfect state. It may well be a comfortable abode, a place where creature comforts abound, and where there is much quiet peace of mind; but those who dwell in such an atmosphere the hidden sweetness of home will never touch. There will be heart-hunger and vague discontents, which puzzle and irritate, and which only the sunshine of love can dispel.

Home-making, like the other arts, is with some an inborn gift,—the secret of making others happy, of conferring blessings, of scattering the sunny *largesse* of love everywhere, is as natural to some as to breathe. Such sweet souls are to be envied, as are those whose happy lot it is to dwell with them. But, at the same time, perhaps they are not so deserving of our admiration and respect as some who, in order to confer happiness on others, themselves undergo what is to them mental and moral privation, who day by day have to keep a curb on themselves in order to crucify the "natural man."

It is possible, even for some whom Nature has not endowed with her loveliest gifts, to cultivate that spirit in which is hidden the whole secret of home happiness. It is the spirit of unselfishness. No selfish man or woman has the power to make a happy home.

By selfish, I mean giving prominence always to the demands and interests of self, to the detriment or exclusion of the interests and even the rights of others. It is possible, however, for a selfish person to possess a certain superficial gift of sunshine, which creates for the time being a pleasant atmosphere, which can deceive those who come casually into contact with him; but those who see him in all his moods are not deceived. They know by experience that a peaceful and endurable environment can only be secured and maintained by a constant pandering to his whims and ways. He must be studied, not at an odd time, but continuously and systematically, or woe betide the happiness of home!

When this element is conspicuous in the woman who rules the household, then that household deserves our pity. A selfish woman is more selfish, if I may so put it, than a selfish man. Her tyranny is more petty and more relentless. She exercises it in those countless trifling things which, insignificant in themselves, yet possess the power to make life almost insufferable. Sometimes she is fretful and complaining, on the outlook for slights and injuries, so suspicious of those surrounding her that they feel themselves perpetually on the brink of a volcano. Or she is meek and martyred, bearing the buffets of a rude world and unkind relatives with pious resignation; or self-righteous and complacent, convinced that she and she alone knows and does the proper thing, and requiring absolutely that all within her jurisdiction should see eye to eye with her.

It is no slight, insignificant domain, this kingdom of home, in which the woman reigns. In one family there are sure to be diversities of dispositions and contrasts of character most perplexing and difficult to deal with. She needs so much wisdom, patience, and tact that sometimes her heart fails her at the varied requirements she is expected to meet, and to meet both capably and cheerfully. If she has been herself trained in a well-ordered home, so much the better for her. She has her model to copy, and her opportunities before her to improve upon it.

Every home is bound to bear the impress of the individuality which guides it. If it be a weak and colourless individuality, then so much the worse for the home, which must be its reflex.

This fact has, I think, something solemn in it for women, and it is somewhat saddening that so many look upon the responsibilities that home-making entails without the smallest consideration. Verily fools rush in where angels fear to tread! If they think of the responsibility at all, they comfort themselves with the delusion that it is every woman's natural gift to keep house; but housekeeping and home-making are two different things, though each is dependent on the other.

This thoughtlessness, which results in much needless domestic misery, is the less excusable because we hear and read so much about the inestimable value of home influences, the powerful and permanent nature of early impressions, even if we are not ourselves living examples of the same. Let us each examine our own heart and mind, and just ask ourselves how much we owe to the influences surrounding early life, and how much more vivid are the lessons and impressions of childhood compared with those of a later date. The contemplation is bound to astonish us, and if it does not awaken in us a higher sense of responsibility regarding those who are under the direct sway of our influence, then there is something amiss with our ideal of life and its purpose.

VI. KEEPING THE
HOUSE

Making the home and keeping the house are two different things, though closely allied. Having considered the graces of mind and heart which so largely contribute to the successful art of home-making, it is not less necessary that we now devote our attention to the more practical, and certainly not less important, quality of housekeeping.

Ignorance of the prosaic details of housekeeping is the primary cause of much of the domestic worry and discomfort that exist, to say nothing of the more serious discords that may arise from such a defect in the fitness of the woman supposed to be the home-maker.

For such ignorance, or lack of fitness, to use a milder term, there does not appear to me to be any excuse; it is so needless, so often wilful.

Some blame careless, indifferent mothers, who do not seem to have profited by their own experience, but allow their daughters to grow up in idleness, and launch them on the sea of matrimony with a very faint idea of what is required of them in their new sphere.

It is very reprehensible conduct on the part of such mothers, and if in a short time the bright sky of their daughters' happiness begins to cloud a little, they need not wonder or feel aggrieved. A man is quite justified in expecting and exacting a moderate degree of comfort at least in his own house, and if it is not forthcoming may be forgiven a complaint. He is to be pitied, but his unhappy wife much more deserves our pity, since she finds herself amid a sea of troubles, at the mercy of her servants, if she possesses them; and if moderate circumstances necessitate the performance of the bulk of household duties, then her predicament is melancholy indeed.

To revert again to our Angelina and Edwin of the comic papers, we have the threadbare jokes at the expense of the new husband subjected to the ordeal of Angelina's awful cooking. At first he is forbearing and encouraging; but in the end, when no improvement is visible, the honeymoon begins to wane much more rapidly than either anticipated. Edwin becomes sulky, discontented, and complaining; Angelina tearful or indignant, as her temperament dictates, but equally and miserably helpless.

The chances are that time will not improve but rather aggravate her troubles, especially if the cares of motherhood be added to those of wifehood, which she finds quite enough for her capacities.

True, some women have a clever knack of adapting themselves readily to every circumstance, and pick up knowledge with amazing rapidity. If they are by nature housewifely women, they will triumph over the faults of their early training, and after sundry mistakes and a good deal of unnecessary expenditure may develop into fairly competent housewives.

But it is a dangerous and trying experiment, which ought not to be made, because there is absolutely no need for it. It is the duty of every mother who has daughters entrusted to her care to begin early to train them in domestic work. That there are servants in the house need be no obstacle in the way. There are silly domestics who resent what they call the "meddling" of young ladies in the kitchen; but no wise woman will allow that to trouble her, but will take care to show her young daughters, as time and opportunity offer, every secret contained in the domestic *répertoire*.

One of the primary lessons to be learned in this housekeeping art is that of method; viz.—a place for everything, and a time. It is the key to all domestic comfort. Most of us are familiar with at least one household where the genius of method is conspicuous by its absence; where regularity and punctuality are unobserved, if not unknown. The household governed by a woman without method is to be pitied. Her husband is a stranger to the comfort of a well-ordered home; and her children, if she has any, hang as they grow, as the Scotch say; while her servants, having nobody to guide them, become careless and indifferent, and so suffer injustice at her hands.

It is such women who are loudest in complaints against servants, and who are in a state of perpetual warfare against the class. Of course this method must be kept within bounds, and not carried to excess, thereby becoming an evil instead of an unmixed good.

We are familiar with that other type of women, who make their housekeeping an idol, at whose shrine they perpetually worship, regardless of the comfort of those under their roof-tree. With them it is a perpetual cleaning day, and woe betide the luckless offender who has the misfortune to mar, if ever so slightly, the immaculate cleanliness of that abode! He is likely to have his fault brought home to him in no measured terms.

The woman possessed of the cleaning mania, who goes to bed to dream of carpet-beating and furniture polish, and who rises to carry her dreams into execution, is quite as objectionable in her way as the woman who never cleans, and for whom the word dirt has no horrors. Although it is doubtless pleasant to feel assured that no microbe-producing speck can possibly lurk in any corner of the house, and to be certain that food and everything pertaining to it is perfect so far as cleanliness is concerned, there is a sense of insecurity and unrest in the abode of the over-particular woman which often develops into positive misery and discomfort. It is the sort of discomfort specially distasteful to the male portion of mankind. Although they may be compelled to admit, when brought to bay, that "cleaning" is a necessary evil, it requires a superhuman amount of persuasion to make them see any good in it. The way women revel, or appear to revel, in the chaos of a house turned topsy-turvy is to them the darkest of all mysteries. It is long since they were compelled to treat it as a conundrum, and give it up.

I think, however, that, with few exceptions, women dislike the periodical household earthquake quite as much as men, and dread its approach. The housekeeper who considers the comfort of those about her will do her utmost to rob it of its horrors. This can be done by a judicious planning, and by resort to the method of which we spoke in the last chapter.

Let "One room at a time" be her motto, and then the inmates of the house will not be made to feel that they are quite in the way, and have no abiding-place on the face of the earth.

This may involve a little more work, and a great deal of patience; but she will have her reward in the grateful appreciation of those for whom she makes home such a happy and restful place.

VII. THE TRUEST
ECONOMY

In these days many new phrases have been coined to give expression and significance to old truths; thus we hear of the "sin of cheapness," the fault attributed to those shortsighted bargain-hunters who waste time and energy and money hunting the length and breadth of the land for the cheapest market. The true and competent housekeeper knows that there is no economy in this method of marketing, but the reverse.

Of course, where the family is large and the resources limited, it is absolutely incumbent on the purveyor to seek the most moderate market; and those of us who dwell in cities know that prices vary with localities, and that West-enders must pay a West-end price. But it is reprehensible always to hunt for cheap things simply because they are cheap, because we ought not to forget that this very cheapness has caused suffering, or at least deprivation, somewhere, since it would appear that some things are absolutely offered at prices under the cost of production.

In the matter of food, so important a factor in the health and well-being of the family, it can seldom be a saving to buy in the cheap market, because cheapness there is too often a synonymous term with unwholesomeness; and a small quantity of the very best will undoubtedly afford more sustenance than an unlimited supply of inferior quality. In small and working-class homes the tea and tinned-food grievance is an old one, but one which does not appear to be in the way of mending.

If the wives and mothers of the working-class could only have it demonstrated to them, beyond all question, that a small piece of excellent fresh beef, made into a wholesome soup flavoured with vegetables, would give three times the nourishment of this tinned stuff, which, good enough as an occasional stand-by, has become the curse and the tyrant of the lazy and thriftless housewife, what a step in the right direction that would be! The mere salting and preserving process destroys the most valuable nutritive elements of the meat; and though it may be tasty and palatable, it is practically useless as a strength-producer or strength-imparter.

Milk, too, we fear has not its proper place in very many homes where children abound; though no mother of even ordinary intelligence can shut her eyes to the fact that it is Nature's own food for her children in their early years, when it is so important to build up the elements of a strong constitution. I would here put in a plea for oatmeal, in former days the backbone of my country's food, and which has of late years fallen sadly into disuse, especially in quarters where its very cheapness and absolute wholesomeness recommend it as *the* food *par excellence* for old and young. We have replaced it with tea and toast, to the great detriment of limb and muscle and digestive power. It is in the palace now we find oatmeal accorded its rightful place, not in the cottage; and the change is to be deplored.

Regularity in meals is another thing the wise housekeeper will insist upon in her abode. Regularity and punctuality, how delightful they are, and how they ease the roll of the domestic wheels! A punctual and tidy woman makes a punctual and tidy home. We know the type who dawdles away the forenoon in idle talk or listless indolence, and rushes to prepare a hasty and only half-cooked meal when perhaps her husband or children are on their way home from school or workshop; and this is a very fruitful cause of domestic dispeace, and at the root even of much of the intemperance which has ruined so many homes. If a man has no comfort at his own fireside, then he is compelled in self-defence to seek it elsewhere.

To recur to the question of buying in cheap markets, the principle that what is good and costs something to begin with will inevitably prove the cheapest in the end is even more clearly demonstrated in the matter of clothing than of food. The best will always wear and look the best, even when it has grown threadbare. Then when we hear so constantly of the appalling misery endured by men and women who make the garments sold in the cheap shops, we are bound to feel that these things are offered at a price which is the cost of flesh and blood. This is a very pressing question, and one which many Christian people do not lay to heart. There appears to be in every human breast the instinct of the bargain-hunter, and there is a placid satisfaction in having got something at an exceptionally low price which charms the finer sensibilities.

To gratify this peculiar and morbid craving, witness the system of buying and selling which prevails in Italy; the shopkeepers there, with few exceptions, invariably asking double the money they are willing to accept. And to this craving in our own country is due the system of all cheap sales in the shops, and mock auctions in the sale-rooms, in which many a shortsighted person of both sexes fritter away both time and money. It is a rotten system, and shows that there is great need for reform in this matter of buying and selling, which occupies so much of our time, means, and thought.

All good housekeepers know that those who buy in the ready-money market fare best; and besides, the paying out of ready-money is undoubtedly a check on expenditure, and is to be specially recommended to people of small means. It is easy and tempting to give an order, and though it can no doubt be paid for sooner or later, somehow the sum always seems to assume larger proportions as time goes on. We very seldom get in a bill for a less amount than we expect. My own view of the case is, that I grudge to pay for food after it is eaten, or clothes after they are worn; and in my own housekeeping I have found ready-money, or, at the outside, weekly accounts, the best arrangement, to which I adhere without any exceptions. Short accounts, also, give one another advantage, the choice of all markets. Thus the money is laid out to the best possible advantage, and the highest value obtained.

All thrifty and far-seeing housekeepers know that it is cheaper to buy certain household stores, as sugar, butter, flour, soap, etc., in quantities, provided there is a suitable storeroom where the things will be kept in good condition. There are indeed innumerable methods whereby the good housewife can save her coppers and her shillings, and a wise woman is she who takes advantage of them to the utmost.

This art of housekeeping is not learned in a day; those of us who have been engaged in it for years are constantly finding out how little we know, and how far we are, after all, from perfection.

It requires a clever woman to keep house; and as I said before there is ample scope, even within the four walls of a house (a sphere which some affect to despise), for the exercise of originality, organising power, administrative ability. And to the majority of women I would fain believe it is the most interesting and satisfactory of all feminine occupations.

VIII. ON KEEPING UP APPEARANCES

In these very words lurks a danger likely to beset our young couple, on the very threshold of their career.

All eyes are upon them, of course; their house and all it contains, their way of life, the position they take up and maintain, are, for the time being, topics of intense concern to all who know them, and to many who do not. There is no doubt that we need to go back in some degree to the simpler way of life in vogue in the days of our grandmothers; that pretentiousness and extravagance have reached a point which is almost unendurable. We are constantly being informed by statistics which cannot be questioned that the marriage rate is decreasing; and we know that in our own circles the number of marriageable girls and marriageable youths who for some inexplicable reason *don't* marry is very great.

What *is* the reason? Is the age of romance over? is it impossible any longer to conjure with the words love and marriage in the garden of youth? or is it that our young people are less brave and enduring, that they shrink from the added responsibility, care, and self-denial involved in the double life? My own view is that this pretentiousness and desire for display is at the bottom of it; that young people want to begin where their fathers and mothers left off, and that courage is lacking to take a step down and begin together on the lowest rung of the ladder.

I have heard many young men say that they are afraid to ask girls to leave the luxury and comfort of their father's house, and to enter a plainer home, where they will have less luxury and more care; and though I grant that there are many girls who would shrink from the ordeal, and who prefer the indolent ease of single blessedness to the cares of matrimony on limited means, yet have I been tempted sometimes, looking at these young men, to wonder in my soul whether it was not *they* who shrank from the plain home and the increased responsibility marriage involves. The salary sufficient for the comfort and mild luxury of one is scarcely elastic enough for two.

It would mean giving up a good many things; it would mean fewer cigars, fewer new suits, fewer first nights at the theatre,— in fact, a general modification of luxuries which he has begun to regard as indispensable; and he asks himself, Is the game worth the candle? His answer is, No. And so he drifts out of young manhood into bachelor middle age, passing unscathed through many flirtations, becoming encrusted with selfish ideas and selfish aims, and gradually less fit for domestic life. And all the time, while he imagines he has a fine time of it, he has missed the chief joy, the highest meaning of life.

The conditions of modern life are certainly harder than they were. Competition in every profession and calling is so enormous that remuneration has necessarily fallen; and it is a problem to many how single life is to be respectably maintained, let alone double. Then the invasions of women into almost every domain of man's work is somewhat serious in its consequences to men. A woman can be got to do a certain thing as quickly, correctly, and efficiently as a man; therefore the man goes to the wall. While we are glad to see the position of woman improve, and the value of her labour in the markets of the world increase, we are perplexed as to the effect of this better condition of things on the position of men. The situation is full of perplexities, strained to the utmost.

There is no doubt whatever that this improvement in the position of woman, the increased opportunities afforded her of making a respectable livelihood, has had, and is having, its serious effect in the marriage market. A single woman in a good situation, the duties of which she has strength of body and strength of mind to perform, is a very independent being, and in contrast with many of her married sisters a person to be envied. She has her hours, for one thing; there is no prospect of an eight hours' day for the married woman with a family to superintend. Then she, having earned her own money, can spend it as she likes—and has to give account of it only to herself; and she is free from the physical trials and disabilities consequent upon marriage and maternity. If you tell her that the sweet fulness of married life, its multiplied joys, amply compensate for the troubles, she will shake her head and want proof.

Altogether, the outlook matrimonial is not very bright. Now, while we deplore, as a serious evil, hasty, improvident, ill-considered marriages, and hold that their consequences are very sad, we would also, scarcely less seriously, deplore that over-cautiousness which is reducing the marriage rate in quarters where it ought not to be reduced,—our lower middle-class, which is the backbone of society. There is no fear of a serious reduction in other quarters: where there is no responsibility felt, there is none to shirk; and so, among the very poor, children are multiplied, and obligations increased, without any thought for the morrow, or concern for future provision. There is a very supreme kind of selfishness in this over-cautiousness which is not delightful to contemplate, the fear lest self should be inconvenienced or deprived in the very slightest degree; and all this does not tend to the highest development of human nature, but rather the reverse, since the spirit of self-denial and self-sacrifice is one of the loveliest attributes of human character.

That it is possible for two people to live together almost as cheaply as one, and, if the wife be careful, thrifty, and managing, with a great deal more comfort, is hardly disputed; and surely love is yet strong enough to take its chance of falling on evil days, and when they come of making the best of them. Our girls must exhibit less frivolity, less devotion to dress and idle amusements, if they wish for homes of their own; because at present it is partly true that men are afraid to take the risk and responsibility of them as partners in life.

And this brings us back to the heading of our chapter, the subject of keeping up appearances. This fearful rivalry to make the greatest show on inadequate means, to outshine our neighbours in house and dress and everything else, is really a tremendous evil, the scourge of many middle-class families. And what, after all, is its aim or outcome; what its rewards?

To begin with, it is a pandering, pure and simple, to the baser part of human nature— the desire to out-rival your neighbour, to be able to soar over him at any price; and more, it is both hypocritical and immoral. Hypocritical, because it is pure pretence to a station which has no means to support it; and immoral, because you cannot afford to pay for it, and thereby suffering is entailed somewhere and somehow. How many of us number among our acquaintances (if not absolutely guilty ourselves), persons who, possessed of a small and limited income, live in a large house, the rent of which is a kind of sword of Damocles hanging over them for ever?

You know them by their hunted, eager, restless look, which tells of inward dispeace, of worry too great almost to be borne. Their servants do not stay long, perhaps because the larder of the big house is kept very bare, and comfort is sacrificed to outside show. They never have anything to give away, and their excuse is that they do not believe in indiscriminate charity. And they look back with a painful longing, never expressed, however, to the days when they lived at peace in a little house, and had enough and to spare for man and beast, and a penny for the beggar at the gate. The big house is but one thing; the struggle to keep up appearances is observed in many other ways—in expensive and not always efficient education of the children, in party-giving, extravagant dress, frequent going out of town, and many others too numerous to mention. And what, after all, is the advantage of it? Is there any advantage gained? You may succeed in exciting in the breast of your neighbour a bitter envy which will probably find expression in some such remark as this—"I only hope it is all paid for."

And you never will have any peace of mind, without which the outward trappings are but a mockery.

Oh, let us be simpler! Let us at least not pretend to be what we are not. In a word, let us not try to humbug ourselves and the world at large.

IX. MOTHERHOOD

It is a great theme, which I approach with fear and trembling; yet—is the home complete without the child? Can even an unpretentious book of this sort be written without some attempted treatment of the same?

The first year of married life is often very full, as well as specially trying, a record of new and very crucial experiences such as are bound to prove the grit of our young housekeeper. She has many things to learn in her new sphere, both in the department of ethics as well as of housekeeping. She has a husband to study, for even though they have seen a great deal of each other before marriage, there yet remains much to learn of many little peculiarities before undreamed of, which in the full glare and test of daily life sometimes stand out with a certain unpleasant prominence, which both find trying. There are new tastes to discover and consider, new likes and dislikes to be studied—in a word, the situation is a severe ordeal, especially if our young wife be very young and inexperienced. Of course she has an adoring and approving love to aid her, and all her efforts to please will be appreciated at their full value, and perhaps a little over, and that is much.

If in addition to all the trying amenities of her new position there be added early in her married life the prospect of motherhood, with its attendant cares, anxieties, and fears, then our young housekeeper may be granted to have hand and heart full. That it is a prospect full of joy and satisfaction, the realisation of a sweet and secret hope, nobody will deny. There are a few women, we are told, who do not desire motherhood, preferring the greater freedom and ease of childless wifehood; but it is not of such we seek to write, because the vast majority agree with me that motherhood is the crown of marriage, as well as the sweetest of all bonds between husband and wife.

It is the great, almost awful, responsibility of this bond which makes thinking people deplore the prevalence of early and improvident marriage between persons who seem to lack entirely this sense of responsibility, and who undertake the most solemn duties in the same flippant mood as they go out on a day's enjoyment. The idea that they have in their power the making and marring of a human soul, to say nothing of the influences which in fulness of time must go forth from that same soul, does not trouble them, or indeed exist for them at all. They have no ideas—they never think. If the child comes, good and well—it has to be provided for; welcome or unwelcome it arrives; and is tolerated or rejoiced over as the case may be.

We need a great deal of educating on this particular point, and the fact that a child may have rights before it is born is one which presses home to the heart of every man and woman who may give the matter any serious attention whatsoever.

If we marry, then as surely do we undertake the possible obligations of parentage; and if we do not see that we are fit physically, mentally, and morally for this undoubtedly greatest of all human obligations, then are we blameworthy, and answerable to God and man for our shortcomings.

Heroism is a word to stir the highest enthusiasm in every heart, and we Britons are not supposed to lack in that glorious quality. While not despising nor making light of that heroism which shows an unflinching front on the battlefield, or in the face of any danger, and while recognising also and glorying in that other heroism of which the world hears less, but which is nevertheless very rich and far-reaching in results—I mean that brave heart which does not sink under adverse circumstances, which makes the best of everything, which can do, dare, and suffer for others, without notice or applause—there is yet another phase of heroism of which the world knows not at all, but which in my estimation is as great, if not greater, than any of these. It is a delicate theme, and yet in such a book as this are we not justified in touching upon it, reverently and tenderly as it deserves? There are some—more, I believe, than we dream of—who, being afflicted physically or mentally, and who, fearing some hereditary moral taint for which they have to suffer, though entirely blameless, deliberately abstain from marriage for the highest of all reasons—that they fear to perpetuate in their own children the weaknesses which are already so stupendous a curse to mankind. Oh that such examples could be multiplied, and that we were once thoroughly awakened to the solemn significance of the fact that the sins of the fathers are visited on the children!

But when we look around we see the innocent made to suffer daily for the guilty; we see children whose lives even in infancy are but a burden to them, and whose later life can only be a cross, and we pray for a great baptism of light on this painful subject, for a great awakening to that personal, individual responsibility which is the only solution of a difficulty which concerns the future and the highest interest of the race.

To return to the question of rights as affecting the unborn babe: the mother has then so much in her power that she can not only determine to a great extent what kind of infancy the child shall have, but also whether her own duties therein shall be heavy or light. By attending strictly to her own health, adhering to natural laws, living simply and wholesomely, she can almost ensure the bodily health of the child; and by keeping her mind calm and even, avoiding worry, and cultivating cheerfulness and contentment, she thus moulds the disposition of the child to a far greater extent than she dreams of. The woman who lives in a condition of perpetual nervous excitement and worry before the birth of her child, who is fretful, complaining, impatient of the discomfort of her condition, need not be much surprised if her baby be fretful and difficult to rear. Of course this is all very easy to write down, and most difficult—in many cases of physical and nervous prostration impossible—to bear in mind; nevertheless, it is worth the trial, worth the self-denial involved, even looking at it from the most selfish standpoint, one's own ultimate comfort and ease. The gain to the child is too great to be estimated.

And surely taking into consideration the enormous number of miserable, weakly babies who have never had a chance, the day of whose birth, like Job's, is sadder than the day of their death, it is not too much to ask from thoughtful Christian women, who at heart feel their responsibility and their high privilege, that nothing shall be lacking on their part to make the child given to them by God a moral, mental, and physical success. We are careful in all other departments of life to try and obtain the best—why not here? Is human life less precious, human souls of less account, than merchandise?

I do not see why mothers should not seek to impress upon their daughters, and fathers upon their sons, as they approach maturity, the solemnity and sacredness of such themes, which involve all that is most important in human life. I consider that the ignorance with which so many young girls are allowed to enter matrimony is nothing short of criminal; and I do not myself see that a plain, straight, loving talk from her mother beforehand, which will prepare her for her new obligations and make them less a surprise and a trial when they come, can possibly take the edge off that exquisite and delicate purity which we would wish to be our daughters' outstanding characteristic, and which every right-thinking man desires in his wife. There are many who do not share this opinion, and hold that the wall of reserve should never be broken. But the issues are great, and I cannot but think that in this case ignorance is more likely to be fruitful of anxiety and foreboding, to say nothing of mistakes, than is a little knowledge wisely imparted by those whom experience has taught.

X. THE SON IN THE
HOME

The son is peculiarly the mother's child, and the bond between them, seen at its best, is one of the loveliest, and, to the woman who has suffered for her firstborn, one of the most soul-satisfying on earth. I suppose most women given choice would wish their firstborn to be a son; and her pride in the boy as he grows in grace and strength and manliness is a very exquisite thing in the mother.

As a rule, a boy is more difficult to rear. He has more strength of limb and will, and shows earlier, perhaps, the desire to be master of the whole situation, as very often he is. It is amazing at how early an age a child can begin to discern between the firm will and the weak will of those who guide him, and to profit thereby; and she is a wise woman who begins as she means to end, and who teaches her child that her decision is absolute from the earliest stage. The moment he begins to understand that though you say no a yell will probably convert it into a yes, your occupation is gone, so to speak—you have lost your hold, and Baby is master of the situation and of you.

There is no doubt, I think, that the woman who has a nurse to relieve her of the child has a better chance than the one who has to fight the battle single-handed—for this reason, that extreme weariness of body, which nothing brings about more quickly than the perpetual care of a baby, is apt to weaken the will; the desire for peace at any price becomes too great to be resisted, and so the citadel is lost. It is impossible also for the ordinary woman, who has the care of a baby all day long, in addition to a multitude of other duties, not to become nervous, irritable, and excitable, and the probability is that the child becomes a reflex of herself. I know of no more self-denying and harassing life than that of the mother of many children, whose limited means prohibit much assistance in her labours. It would require the strength of a Hercules and the patience of a Job. Yet how many go on from day to day with an uncomplaining and heroic cheerfulness which does not strike the onlooker, simply because it is so common, like the toothache, that it attracts but little sympathy or attention.

In one day such a mother may win moral victories beside which the brilliant engagements of the battlefield would pale. It is not one that she has to consider and contend with, but many; the diversity of disposition in one family is truly amazing, and affords a most interesting psychological study. If she be a thoughtful and conscientious woman she knows that she is sowing the seeds of future good and ill, that early impressions are never erased, and that her own influence is the one which will leave the strongest, the most indelible mark on the future of the little ones she has under her wing. To this there is no exception whatever; it is a fact nobody attempts to dispute. Who shall say, then—who shall dare to say—that a woman's work is slight, her sphere narrow, her influence feeble? Have we not yet with us the proverb, "She who rocks the cradle rules the world"? as true to-day as it was a hundred years ago, as it will be in a hundred years to come.

But though the anxieties and responsibilities of the nursery are great, they increase, especially in the case of some, as the years go by; though as the boy grows older his mother may be somewhat relieved by the wise guidance of the father. There comes a time when the lad wants to emancipate himself from his mother's jurisdiction, and begins to look to his father, seeing in him the image of what he may yet become. He will not love his mother any less, but he will be impatient a little, perhaps, of her careful supervision; he wants to be a man, to imitate his father, to show that he is a being of another order. It is always amusing to look on at this subtle and inevitable change, but sometimes touching as well. It is the strong soul seeking his heritage, the first stirring of manhood in the boy, who will never be other than a bairn to his mother. Happy then the mother, blessed the boy, who has a good, wise, and tender father to take him by the hand, and show him at this critical stage the beauty of a noble, pure, and honest manhood, and how great is its power to bless the world.

There are some men who never grow old, who, while doing a man's part better than most in the world, keep the child-heart pure within them. Happy are the children who call them father! The ideal father (since we are writing of what we all know to be the highest in home relationship, we may call him so) will be a boy in the midst of his boys all his days; he will share the pastimes, the interests, the absorbing occupations of his boys, in the schoolroom and the recreation-ground, just as he did not disdain to join sometimes in the frolic of the nursery. He will understand cricket and football, and hounds and hares, and know all the little points of schoolboy honour, so that he may at once grasp the situation when his lad brings his grievance or his tale of victory to him. And through it all, without preaching, which the soul of the average boy abhors, he will seek to inculcate the highest moral lessons, thus accentuating and deepening the teaching of the nursery still fresh in the boy's mind.

This is the ideal which we would wish to see in every home, but the real is rather different, and sometimes perplexing to deal with. We have seen homes where the boys do not "get on" with their father, who seem to rub each other the wrong way, and to have no sort of kinship with each other—in a word, who are not chums, which is a boy's definition of the jolliest possible relationship, and which is very beautiful existing between father and son. But there are fathers who have no patience with the boy who, feeling in him the promptings of a larger life, begins to give himself little airs, and to adopt a manly and masterful manner; no sympathy with his desire for freedom; and who, instead of wisely guiding all these accompaniments of young manhood into fresh and legitimate channels, seeks to curb them, to restrain every impulse, and to enforce an authority the boy does not understand, and inwardly, if not outwardly, kicks against.

I know many mothers who have difficulty in pouring oil on such troubled waters, and who see that the father and the boy do not understand each other, and cannot get on— and she is powerless to help. Out of this strained relationship many evils may arise. The young heart, bounding with a thousand buoyant impulses, eager to see life and taste its every cup, deprived of sympathy and outlet, and thrown back upon itself, becomes reserved, self-contained, and morbid. Then, again, there is a temptation to concealment, and even to prevarication, over mere trifles. When censure is feared— and the young heart is fearfully sensitive— little fibs are told to escape it, and so a great moral wrong is inflicted, which can undoubtedly be laid at the unsympathetic parent's door.

The mother, by reason of her gentler nature (to which, of course, there are the usual exceptions), is not so feared, and is made the go-between.

"Mother, will *you* ask father for so-and-so?" is an everyday question in many homes; and why should it be? Why should sympathy and confidence be less full and sweet between father and son than between mother and son? Nay, rather, it might be fuller, since the father, being of the same sex, can the better understand the boy nature, making allowance for its failings, which were also his, if, indeed, they are not in an aggravated form still characteristic of him. Some men forget that they have ever been young; looking at them and witnessing their conduct in certain circumstances, one finds it difficult to believe that they ever *were* young. They have been fossils from their birth. That is the grand mistake—to fix such a great gulf betwixt youth and maturity that nothing can bridge it. It is more love, more sympathy we want; it is the dearth of it that is the curse of the world. Yet how dare we, being responsible for the advent of the child into the world, deny him his heritage, starve his heart of its right to our affection and regard? The Lord sent him? Well, He did undoubtedly, and His commands with the gift. There is no hesitation or ambiguity about the Lord's mandate regarding little children.

In homes where this lovely sympathy exists, anxiety regarding the moral welfare of the boy is reduced to a minimum. Where the youth can come to his mother, and still better to his father, in every dilemma, sure of advice and aid, he will not go very far wrong. The world is full of pitfalls, and it is sure nothing short of the grace of God can keep young manhood in the right way; but very certain am I that parents have much, ay, more than they dream of in their power.

Let them at least see to it that they do not fall short. Let the boy feel that the home is his, that his friends are welcome to it, and that he need not go out always to seek liberty and enjoyment. In one word, let him have room to breathe and to live, and the chances are that he will repay you by becoming all you could desire even in your fondest dreams.

XI. THE DAUGHTER IN THE HOME

The home is incomplete without the daughter, the sweet little baby who from the first entwined herself about her parents' hearts; and who, as she grows in beauty, is a source of constant joy and pride, not quite untouched by anxiety. For when we have educated our sons and done for them all we possibly can, they can, as a rule, stand on their own sturdy legs, and take their own place in the world, we looking on with pride if they adorn it well— with sadness if they fall short. We do not love them less, but they sooner place themselves beyond our jurisdiction, and responsibility concerning them is sooner at an end. With the daughters it is different. As the old rhyme says—

"A son is a son till he gets him a wife, A daughter's a daughter to the end of her life,"

words which just express the whole situation. Even after she marries our anxiety and loving concern for her in her new sphere quite equals the old; her little children, reminding us of what she was once to us, are dear to us in a way our son's children can never be. It seems a strange anomaly, yet will most mothers bear me out in what I say.

A home where there are many boys and no girls is a jolly, healthy, happy household enough, but it lacks something, a gentler element, which the boys miss keenly, though they may not even be conscious of it. It is a great misfortune for boys to have no sisters, because in the family circle, where they grow up side by side, they acquire a knowledge of girl-nature which is invaluable to them when they begin to take an interest in that interesting personage, "another fellow's sister." And *vice versâ*—girls brought up in a brotherless home have no opportunity of studying boy-nature, and are apt to take a very prim, narrow view of the same. The ideal family is the one judiciously mixed, where boys and girls rub shoulders and carry on their little campaigns, entering into each other's pursuits and being chums all round. It is good for both.

As I said before, girls, even in infancy, are more easily managed and reared than boys, the usual exceptions being allowed; and the same may be said of them as they grow older. They are more docile, more amenable to control, and their animal spirits, dependent on bodily organisation, are not usually so obstreperous. It is astonishing how soon a little girl becomes a companionable creature; she develops at a much earlier age than her brothers. Of course there are great differences. We have the tomboy, never still, more interested in her brothers' pranks than in the sober frolics of girls—dolls have no charm for her; yet the curious thing is that the tomboy has been known to develop into the extraordinarily successful wife and mother, her very energies of mind and body, when mellowed by experience, proving invaluable to her in her new sphere.

I have often thought that an interesting article might be written on the place and power of dolls in the early life of women; it is such an interesting study to watch the different grades of interest taken in them by different children. To some they are real flesh and blood, treated as such, fondled over and considered quite as much as any living baby, invested with aches and pains, tempers and troubles, and subjected to a regular system of reward and punishment; while to others they are mere toys, which serve only to beguile the tedium of a rainy day. Then there are the few who regard them as mere objects for scorn and hatred; and when they do not ignore them, maltreat them mercilessly.

The small girl who hates dolls, and dubs them as stupid things, is apt to be a little troublesome to amuse, though it is also quite possible that she may possess a very original mind, which strikes out a new path even in amusement for itself.

Some little boys who afterwards became good and noble men have not disdained dolls as a baby amusement, and you generally find that the small boy who takes a kind interest in his sister's dolls, and who does not spend his leisure in concocting schemes for their torture and dismemberment, has the fatherly instinct very strongly developed, and will in his own home be tenderly devoted to his children.

Boys ought to be taught early the beauty of little kindly attentions and thoughtfulness for others. On no account ought their sisters to be allowed to fetch and carry for them. There may be a system of mutual obligation if you like, but boys of a certain age are apt to become very arbitrary, and to consider their sisters in the light of body servants. By allowing boys to order their sisters about, to bring them things and give in always, you foster a spirit of selfishness, which grows tyrannical as the years go by, and paves the way for some domestic discomfort in a future home which will be beyond your jurisdiction.

They tell us the age of chivalry is dead; and really manners do not seem to be as they were. The changed order of things concerning women, who are no longer cooped up within the four walls of a house, and told that that is their sphere spelled with a very big S, but who are pushing their way steadily to the front in every walk of life, no doubt partly accounts for this; still the lapse of that old-fashioned and gracious courtesy of men to women is to be deplored, and I cannot but think that we who have raw material to work upon in the nursery might do something to restore it. We cannot afford to lose any of the graces of life. Heaven knows things are reduced to a prosaic enough level with us in these days, when the fret and fever seem to leave time for nothing but the barest realities.

As we have already admitted that early impressions and early training never quite lose their hold, so if we teach our boys to be gracious, courteous, considerate always to their sisters because they are little women, some women of a later date will be grateful to us.

The very advanced of our sex have been known to disclaim any desire for such consideration; they want none from the opposite sex, but only room to fight the battle side by side; but we who do not wish to see life robbed of all its grace and courtliness would respectfully insist that this reserve should not be entirely dispensed with. We still like a man to take off his hat to us in the street, instead of jerking his head on one side; we have no objection to the inside of the pavement or the most comfortable seat in carriage or tram, for which we have still a word of appreciative thanks left, though we may thereby show how far we are left behind in the race. I wish to make myself very clear. We do not want our girls to be namby-pamby, selfish, silly creatures, who imagine it is interesting and fascinating to pose as weak, dependent, fluttering creatures; but neither do we want our sons to be boors, and it is in the home where manners as well as morals are formed. So let us not despise the little courtesies which do so much to sweeten daily intercourse, but teach them to the children from the beginning, so that to be chivalrous, courteous, gentle to rich and poor, gentle and simple of both sexes, will become as natural for them as to breathe.

XII. THE EDUCATION
OF OUR DAUGHTERS

Even a very young daughter can be of use to her mother, and her influence felt in the house, if she is taught how. Of course, the first concern, when our little maid gets out of the nursery, is that she should be educated, and her mental powers have the best possible chance of being brought to their full power.

The education of our girls is one of the great questions of the day—engrossing the interest of those in the highest places; and a healthy sign of the times it is. For since it is upon the women of to-day that the future of the race depends, what could be of greater importance than that all her powers, physical, mental, and moral, should be brought as near perfection as possible?

Do I of a set purpose mention the physical first? Yes; because the older I grow the more it comes home to me that unless we have sound and healthy bodies we can but poorly serve our day and generation. Therefore the food the children eat should be one of our chief studies and concerns; because if we can send them out into the world with constitutions built upon a sure and common-sense foundation, it is the best possible service we can render them; and one for which they and theirs will be grateful always.

This question of education is rather a perplexing one, which gives parents a great deal of anxious thought. The present system is undoubtedly a great improvement upon any we have had heretofore, and yet it seems to leave something to be desired. In the board schools, where the bulk of the lower middle-class children are educated, and where tuition is very excellent and thorough, there is yet this drawback,—all are sought to be raised to one dead level, the passing of so many standards being imperative, nor any consideration given to individual capacity or fitness. The inevitable result of this is that the teacher is bound to concentrate his attention on the dull pupils, in order to get them dragged up to the required standard, the bright ones being left pretty much to their own devices. However much he may deplore this, he cannot help himself, since it is upon his percentage of passes that his status as a teacher, to say nothing of his salary, depends. Therefore in some respects the old system of parochial teaching had its advantage over the new.

But it is very specially of the education of the girls we wish to speak, and it is gratifying to observe that many parents are awaking to the absurdity of insisting that their daughters shall acquire a superficial knowledge of certain accomplishments, whatever the bent of their minds. How much money, to say nothing of precious time, has been sacrificed in the vain pursuit of music, that sweetest of the arts; which is so often desecrated and tortured by unwilling and unsympathetic votaries. It very soon becomes evident whether the child has an aptitude for music or not; and if she has not, but finds the study of it an imposition and a trial, what is the use of forcing her to such unwilling drudgery, when very likely she possesses some other aptitude, the cultivation of which will be both profitable and pleasant? How many girls upon whom pounds and pounds have been spent never touch the piano when they are emancipated from schoolroom control; and how much more usefully could both time and money have been employed in the pursuit of something else!

Mothers are beginning to see this, and it is a welcome awakening. So long as our young maiden is occupied with school and lessons, she has not time to learn much else, since it is imperative that she has recreation likewise; it is when she leaves school that the wise mother, having an eye to the future, will at once seek to initiate her into the mysteries of housekeeping. True, she may never have a home of her own; she may be one of those called to labour, perhaps, in the very forefront of the working women outside; but all the same she ought not to be ignorant of what used to be considered the chief, if not the only occupation for women,—she ought to be fit to keep house on the shortest notice. It is a woman's heritage. Whatever she may or may not know, I hold that she ought to acquire a certain amount of domestic knowledge, whether she uses it or not. Most young girls are interested in domestic affairs, and are never happier than when allowed to have their finger in the domestic pie; but in this as in other things a thorough grounding is the most satisfactory.

It is astonishing what undreamed-of qualities a sense of responsibility awakens in a young soul; how the very idea that something depends on her, that she is being trusted, puts our little maid upon her mettle. Therefore it is a good plan to leave to a young daughter some particular duty or duties for which she is entirely responsible.

This may of course be a very slight thing to begin with—the dusting of a room, or the arrangement of flowers or books, or the superintendence of the tea-table; but whatever it is, the mother should insist that it be done regularly and at the appointed time. Thus will she teach her child punctuality and a primary lesson in a method, which is the key to all perfect housekeeping. Of course it is a little trouble to the mother to superintend the performance of such little duties, but she will have her reward in the daily increasing helpfulness of the daughter in the home.

Most young girls, if skilfully dealt with, speedily learn to take a special pride in their own little duties, especially if their efforts be met with appreciation. Never snub a child; the young heart is very sensitive, and takes a long time to forget. Little changes in the domestic routine will be introduced by the wise mother, in order that the work may not become irksome.

Where there are several daughters, it is a good plan for them to exchange their particular duties for a time. Thus, one may assist with the cooking for a week, then change with her sister who has the care and arrangement of the drawing-room or sitting-room, or with the one who helps with the mending. So the daily round would never become monotonous, and by gradual and pleasant degrees a knowledge of the whole system of housekeeping is acquired, which will be simply invaluable to her, whatever her future may be. If the family circumstances demand that she shall go out into the world to earn her living by teaching or typewriting or shopkeeping, the wise mother will not for this reason relax her desire and effort to teach her the art and mystery of housekeeping. True, while she is occupied outside she has little opportunity to learn it, but "where there's a will there's a way"; and though it may not appear at present of much practical value to her, yet she may marry, or have to go to single housekeeping, when the home is no longer open to her. I again insist that it is every woman's duty to know, or to acquire some practical knowledge of housekeeping, so that she may be ready for any emergency. Her fitness for it will be a perpetual source of satisfaction to her, for there is nothing more self-satisfying than to feel that one is capable; it gives confidence, strength, and self-reliance.

One of the very necessary lessons to be taught a young girl is the value of money. The sooner she learns what equivalent in household necessaries money can procure the better. The day may come when the tired mother will be glad to be relieved even of the responsibility of spending, and when, thanks to her own wisdom and foresight, she can place the family purse in younger hands, knowing that the contents will not be recklessly or extravagantly spent. Let our young maiden feel that she is entirely trusted, and that a great deal is expected of her, then will she display qualities undreamed-of. She will be eager to show what she can do; and when the word of encouragement and appreciation is not lacking she will be proud and happy indeed. Of course there are perverse natures, of whom one is tempted at times to despair—irresponsible young persons who would make wild havoc in any establishment left to their care; but I am speaking of the average young girl, who may be expected to be thoughtless and forgetful often, as is the way of youth, but who nevertheless has the makings of a fine, gentle-hearted, noble woman in her.

"What shall we do with our daughters?" is one of the great questions of the day. Formerly marriage was their only destiny; if they missed that, they were supposed to have missed all that was worth the winning here. But that old fallacy is exploded. While still holding that in happy marriage is to be found the fullest and most soul-satisfying life for women, no open-eyed person will deny that a single, independent, and self-respecting life is far preferable to the miserable, starved, inadequate wifehood to which many women are bound. Having dealt in a former chapter with the question of matrimony, I must here avoid repetition, but in connection with this subject of our daughters we must touch upon it once again. The wise mother will rear her daughters to be independent, self-respecting, and, if possible, self-supporting; not hiding from them that she considers a real marriage (not the mockery of it so often seen) the highest destiny for them, but at the same time impressing on them that there are other spheres in which women may be as happy and comfortable, and where they will certainly have less anxiety and care.

The woman who trains her daughters in the belief that marriage is their only end and aim, the very *raison d'être* of their being, is a mistaken, despicable creature, and in all probability her daughters will take after her.

If they do not marry, then what is to become of our daughters? Of late years their path of life has opened up more widely and clearly, and though the avocations open to women are very crowded there is still room for the best equipped. That is the secret,—to bring to the market the highest value only, to render oneself as efficient as nature and circumstances permit. I would have our girls fully comprehend that in this age of unprecedented strain and stress there is absolutely no room for mediocrity, and that they cannot afford to be anything but the most efficient workers in whatever department they have made their own. There is still room for the best, and persevering, conscientious labour, worth the highest market value, sooner or later meets its due appreciation and reward.

XIII. THE SERVANT IN THE HOME

Any little book attempting to treat of home-life must necessarily be incomplete without some reference to the place and power of the servant therein. We housekeepers all know that this servant question is just as pressing as any upon which we have yet touched, and it is one that is with us every day. We cannot rid ourselves of it, even if we would, because it involves so much of our domestic comfort and happiness.

We of modern days are filled with a vague envy when we read of such treasures as Caleb Balderstone, Bell of the Manse, and various other types of a class now, we fear, extinct—the faithful servitor, who lived in the service of one house for generations and desired to die in it. Perhaps such types had their drawbacks likewise, and sometimes presumed past endurance, doing what seemed good in their own eyes, and that alone. But all that could be forgiven, because, weighed in the balance with a lifelong devotion and loyalty and love, they were as nothing. A few Calebs and Bells undoubtedly still exist, but the bulk of modern housekeepers know them not, and regard them as pleasant creatures of fiction, impossible to real life.

Are servants really less efficient, less conscientious, less diligent than they were? Or is it that we expect and exact more? Modern life has undergone such a tremendous change, there have been so many upheavals in relative positions, that we are inclined to think domestic service is now regarded from a very different standpoint than it was fifty, or even twenty, years ago. It is no longer regarded as honourable; those who enter it seem to do so under protest, the result being a most unsatisfactory relation within doors. Some blame education for this; and yet it seems hard to believe that education, the pioneer of progress everywhere and in all ages, should be responsible for such a distorted view. Some will tell us that this very dissatisfaction is a sign of the times, indicating the march of progress towards the time when all men shall be equal, and no more lines of demarcation shall be drawn. Never were wages higher; never, I am very sure, were domestic servants treated with more consideration and respect; and yet the fact remains that girls prefer almost any other occupation to it. They will stand for hours behind a counter, suffering untold tortures from exhaustion and insufficient food, content to receive a mere pittance, and subjected to a system of espionage and bullying far harder to bear than anything found in domestic service; and they will give you as their reasons, in general, these: It is more genteel, they have their evenings and their Sundays free, and they are not required to wear the livery of cap and apron. These are the reasons, then; what are we to make of them?

Can we make domestic service more genteel; give evenings and Sundays free; and are we willing to dispense with the badge distinguishing maid from mistress? These are the questions we have before us, waiting an answer; in that answer perhaps may be found the solution of the whole stupendous difficulty.

I write under one disadvantage. I have never been a domestic servant, and I cannot therefore look at the situation from that particular standpoint; but I have had for some years servants under my roof, and I have my own experiences of these years to guide me from the mistress's point of view. During these years I can truthfully say that I have most conscientiously, kindly, and systematically done my best to make them happy; that I have considered them very often at the expense of my own comfort; and though I have had no startling experiences whatsoever, I am bound to admit that the result on the whole is not particularly encouraging. I have seldom found that corresponding consideration, that devotion to my concerns, that warm personal interest, which make one feel that one has friends in the household. I have had my pound of flesh, nothing more; they have done the work for which they have been paid, sometimes well, but often carelessly; and that is all. When it came to a question of personal consideration, of caring for my substance, looking after my interests as I have honestly tried to look after theirs, I have been disappointed, and now I expect no more, thankful if I have average comfort, and do not have my nerves and temper tried a hundred times a day. This I suppose is the experience of two-thirds of the women who may read this book.

Nobody feels more keenly than I do the monotonous drudgery of a servant's life. Day in, day out, the same weary round; and while the same may be said of all workers, in whatsoever estate they may find themselves, yet is the lot of the domestic servant notoriously a dull routine. I often wonder, indeed, that without that element of personal interest which is the only thing to make the multitudinous and weary round of household duties sweet, or in any way tolerable, she should do it half so well; but, on the other hand, when one thinks of her absolute freedom from care, sordid or otherwise, a feeling of impatience is bound to arise. "All found" is a comprehensive phrase, and it is those who have to "find" it who have the care, the thought, the anxious planning.

How, then, can we establish a better understanding between mistress and maid, how lift this question to its highest platform, and render the service one which will be honoured and sought after, instead of despised, and entered on under compulsion, or as a last resource? I confess, for once, I am baffled completely, and beyond redemption. I have thought of it long and earnestly, have done my best with my own opportunities, and I have no glorified results to offer. I am as others, worried and often weary, and grateful for every small mercy that comes in my way. It seems to me that we want to enlarge our own minds and the minds of those we take into our employ; we need a wider vision, which shall lift us clean above mere petty and selfish concerns. That is a baptism we all need. When shall it descend?

I am forced to this conclusion—that it is this question of all others that is absolutely dependent on the grace of God. We must have the true spirit of Christianity in our kitchens and in our drawing-rooms,—that spirit whose gracious teaching is never ambiguous or difficult to understand; in a word, there is nothing but the Sermon on the Mount will do us any good. Of human preaching, teaching, and writing we have enough and to spare—it does not appear to go home, or to bear any practical fruit.

We can only pray that He, whose great heart is open now as it was then to every human need, will help us to realise our responsibility to each other, will give us new lessons in the law of love, and show us that service is the highest form of praise, and that nothing is really small or mean or despicable, except sin and the littleness of human aims.

All work is honourable, nay, it is the highest calling on earth. It can only be dishonoured in the doing. If each one, master and man, mistress and maid, could adopt this attitude towards their daily duty to the world and to each other, there would be found the solution of the problem vexing the souls of so many at the present day.

XIV. RELIGION IN THE HOME

Perhaps this chapter might more appropriately have been placed at the beginning of the book than at the end, seeing we have in it the root of the whole matter, the key to all happiness, fitness, comfort, and peace. Religion is a word much misunderstood, yet it is given to us in the Epistle of St. James in the clearest, most intelligible language,—"Pure religion and undefiled is to visit the widows and the fatherless in their affliction, and to keep himself unspotted from the world."

It always seems to me that the former part of the injunction is easier than the latter. There is so much in the world with which we must combat, so much that, though we can avoid in one sense, comes so very near to us, that it is well-nigh impossible to keep ourselves unspotted. But though there is a great deal of evil around us, we must not be such cowards as to shrink from facing it, and shut ourselves up in selfish safety, lest it should come near us at all. This is not what the Apostle means, for it is possible to be in the world and yet not of it, it is written too that "to the pure all things are pure." What we have to do is to see that in our inmost thoughts we are pure, not giving lodgment in our mind to any unholy thing which if revealed would bring the blush of shame to our cheek. But in the high standard of personal purity, which we may rightly set up for ourselves, let us not be too arrogant, or forgetful that such as fall away from purity may have been subjected to such terrible temptations as we know nothing of. Let us cultivate more of that Divine compassion towards them which Christ showed of old towards the Magdalene. It is in matters of such immediate and personal interest that the spirit of the religion we profess is to be exhibited,—in a word, we must consecrate all to the high service God requires of us, honouring us in the requirement. We are placed in this world to be happy and useful; and though we are reminded many times by personal sorrows and bereavements that we have no continuing city here, yet the knowledge need not make us gloomy, or restless, or dissatisfied.

In this lovely world, so full of beauty and variety, we are bidden to rejoice; it is for our enjoyment and our use, there is no stint or condition attached to our citizenship of God's earth. Nature is mother to all, and has a message for the meanest and most tried of her children; and it is a message of divinest love. Through Nature, His handmaid, God speaks to us, giving us in the dawn of each new day, in the return of each season, in the shining of the sun and the blessing of the rain, grand and practical lessons in faith, fulfilment of promises which should mean a great deal to us, and teach us more and more to trust Him in all and through all. While we are in the world we have a duty to it, and those who neglect or think lightly of the practical and commonplace requirements of daily life are in the wrong. What is needed is a deepened sense of responsibility concerning the charge God has given us to keep for Him, in the house, the workshop, or the busy mart of life.

It is with the home we have presently to deal; and it is in the home, I think, we need certainly, in as great a degree as elsewhere, all the aid and stimulus religion can give. It teaches us to make the very best of all our circumstances, adverse or pleasant; and aids us to the performance of all duties, however monotonous or irksome in themselves. It is not ours to inquire whether these duties are just what we would desire or choose for ourselves, had choice remained with us. Religion does not consist in the performance of religious ordinances, in conscientious reading of the Word or the utterance of its formal prayers; these are its attributes, its natural outcome, not by any means the thing itself. Religion is, I take it, to be a principle, a powerful guiding motive to direct us in the ordinary affairs of life, and its mainspring is love. Love for whom? For the Lord Jesus. And if we love Him, and truly desire to serve Him, it will be no difficulty for us, but a natural and exquisite result, that we love one another.

Even the enemies of Christ, who deny His divinity, admit the beauty and perfectness of His character, and the unselfishness and holiness of His earthly life. Since these three-and-thirty years He walked with men many new Christs have risen, many new creeds and dogmas been offered for the world's acceptance; but all have passed away, disappeared into nothingness, and Christ remains, the mainstay and salvation of human souls. His teaching is still the very best we can obtain for our guidance here. Take the Sermon on the Mount, for instance. How perfect it is, how comprehensive, how full of little things, and yet how wide-reaching in its limit! There is nothing forgotten; nearly nineteen hundred years old, and yet it is adapted for every need of the human soul. If we could get the spirit of that blessed teaching more firmly planted in our hearts, we could make the world a happier place for ourselves and others. We are all fond of laying plans for the future; and there are few of us who do not at least once a year review the past, and make new resolves for the future. Some of us are constantly taking retrospects, and sometimes feel hopeless. We seem to be making so little progress in that higher life which we desire, and strive after in some degree. In a twofold sense this looking back may be made profitable to us. It must always, unless we are very hard of heart, make us grateful for past mercies; and when we consider how wonderfully and tenderly we have been led through difficulties and trials, or dangers, or guided through the more perilous waters of prosperity and success, it will give us greater heart to go forward to whatever may lie before us. When we look back on lost opportunities, it must make us more watchful of those present with us, and help us to give to each new day as it comes something upon which we shall afterwards look back without regret. The older I grow the more strongly do I feel that religion is a matter of daily living—of practice, not precept; and that unless the Spirit of Christ animate us in all our relations one to the other we name His name in vain. And what a lovely spirit it was, unsullied by any trace of selfishness, gentle, forbearing, long-suffering, just to the last degree!

It is this spirit alone that can sanctify and bless the home, and raise all common life out of a sordid groove; that can make homely things beautiful, and hard things, of which so many meet us on life's road, easier to bear. Oh that we had a larger baptism of it; that we who so long and strive for it could have it always with us! Human nature is so perverse, and self so strong. Yet, even in its weakest efforts, this earnest desire to live the religion Christ has taught us will not go unblessed, but will make its little lesson felt wherever it is found. Because it makes us more self-denying, more charitable, more forbearing in every relation of life, it will make others inquire concerning the hope that is in us.

"In hidden and unnoticed ways; In household work, on common days,"

we may do the Master's work, and make our homes altars to His glory.

We want less talk and more action, less precept and more example, which though reticent of speech is yet eloquent in testimony for good or for evil. So, whatever be our lot or circumstances, whatever our joys and sorrows, our losses or crosses, we may with confidence look ahead, and our great compensation will not be lacking—"She hath done what she could"; and again, "Well done, good and faithful servant: enter thou into the joy of thy Lord."

www.ingramcontent.com/pod-product-compliance
Lightning Source LLC
Chambersburg PA
CBHW062223080426
42734CB00010B/2004